This book is dedicated to my nature-loving husband, Steve.

Thank you for all of your love, encouragement, and support.

And to my daughter, Sarah, your encouragement is immeasurable.

All rights reserved. No part of this publication may be reproduced,
stored in a retrieval system, or transmitted in any form or by any means,
electronic, mechanical, photocopy, recording, or otherwise,
without the prior permission of the author or illustrator,
nor be otherwise circulated in any form of binding or cover
other than that which it is published and
without a similar condition being imposed on the purchaser.
This a work of fiction. Any names, characters, or situations are used fictitiously.
Any resemblance of actual persons living or dead is entirely coincidental.
Copyright
© All Rights Reserved.
®LenaLaRue
©2023 Illustrations. All Rights Reserved.
Published by Wellspring Renewal

ISBN 978-1-959087-03-8 (Paperback)
ISBN 978-1-959087-05-2 (Hardcover)
ISBN 978-1-959087-04-5 (Digital online)
First edition 2023
edited by Amy Wilson
Library of Congress Control Number: 2023909977

Harlan and the Bee

A Children's Book about Compassion and Sharing.

Story by Lena LaRue **Art by Sammie Clark**

Published 2023

There once was a charming flower garden with fragrant red roses,

yellow lilies and bright purple buds of lavender that swayed in

the wind.

The buzz of honeybees filled the air. They flew and hovered from

blossom to blossom to collect pollen. Then they return to their

hive. Each bee had an important job working hard to keep the hive

alive and thriving.

Like the other pollinators, Harlan spent his day flying from one

flower to another. But the sweet sugar water in the hummingbird

feeder was his delight.

It was new to the garden. With no other water source

around, it quenched his thirst throughout the day.

And he did not want to share it.

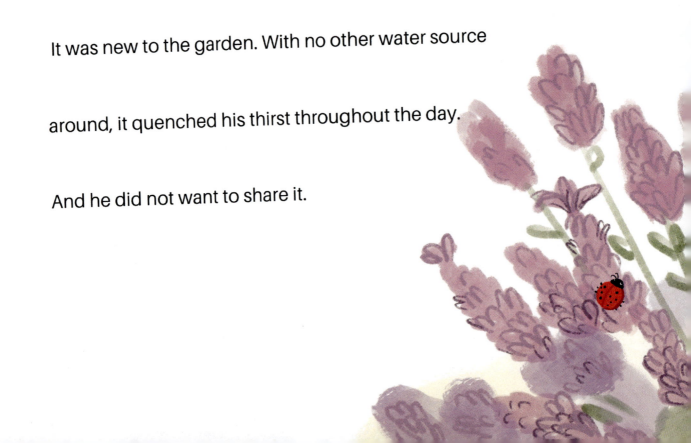

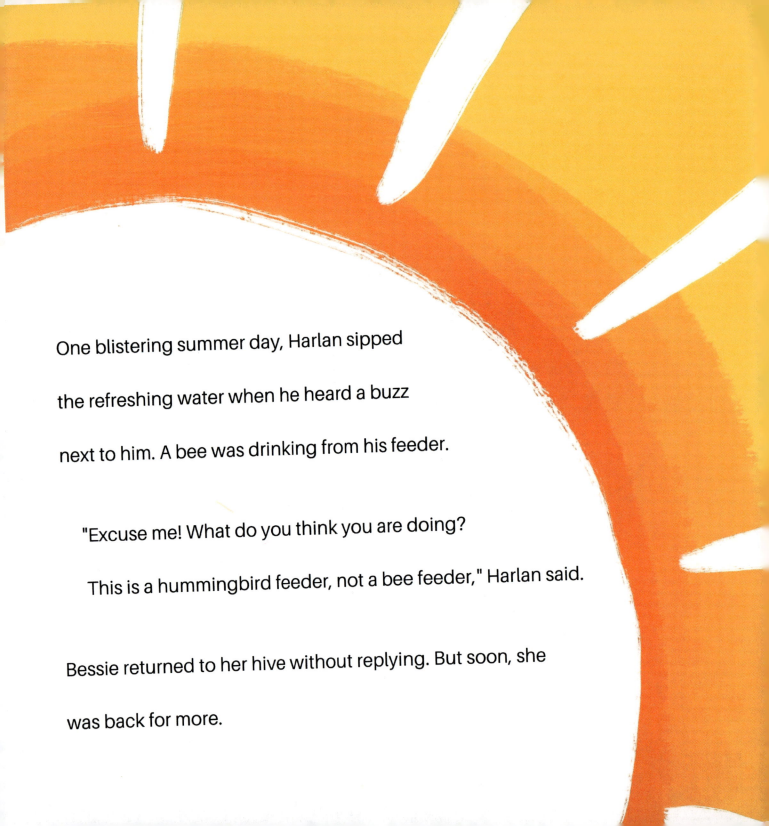

One blistering summer day, Harlan sipped the refreshing water when he heard a buzz next to him. A bee was drinking from his feeder.

"Excuse me! What do you think you are doing? This is a hummingbird feeder, not a bee feeder," Harlan said.

Bessie returned to her hive without replying. But soon, she was back for more.

Who does she think she is? Harlan thought.

He tried to shoo her away with his long beak.

She quickly dodged his movements and rushed

back to the hive.

After his next sip, he noticed she had returned for more.

This has got to stop. There won't be any water left. Thought Harlan.

He was ready to duel. She fended him off with her stinger.

Then she flew back to the hive with her mouth full of water.

What was she doing with his water?

He followed her. There was a line of bees fanning their wings on the edge of the hive. He spotted the *thief* as she darted out and raced back to *his* water trove.

"Hold on!" Harlan said.

"No time to talk. It is too hot. The babies might die!" Bessie said as she slurped a mouthful and buzzed home.

He watched her spit the water onto the hive floor for the other bees.

"Why are you wasting *my* water?" Harlan shouted as he trailed behind her.

"I'm not wasting it," she said.

"I saw you spit out *my* water on the floor of the hive."

Harlan flew between Bessie and the hummingbird feeder.

"If I explain, will you please stop blocking me?"

"The temperature inside the hive is hotter than outside.

If it gets too hot, the larvae babies might die. The fanning bees vibrate their wings to pull out the hot air and draw the cooler air into the hive. But this dries out the honey inside of the honeycomb. We feed the babies honey mixed with pollen.

I leave the water for the worker bees to mix with the honey to feed the babies and cool the hive."

She guzzled more water and flew away.

So, she was not being greedy or wasteful? She was saving lives. Thought Harlan.

When she returned, he was ready.

He flew behind her. After she emptied her water load,

he gently released the water he held in his beak.

Then he carefully fanned the hive.

The surrounding bees were shocked.

They buzzed and cheered.

"Buzz, buzz! Yeah! Woo-hoo! Hooray! Buzz, buzz!"

He smiled and followed the little bee back for more.

It felt good to help. Together, they cooled the hive all day.

At sunset, Bessie stopped and said to Harlan,

"Thank you for your help."

"You are welcome. I'm sorry I was mean to you.

I was wrong to keep the water to myself. I guess everyone

in the garden needs water, don't they?" asked Harlan.

"Yes, every bird, bee, bug and blossom needs water. When you share your water, you are a **water hero,**" said Bessie.

Then she buzzed away. Harlan liked the sound of that.

"See you again tomorrow!" he said.

ABOUT THE AUTHOR

Lena LaRue is passionate about writing children's books comparable to the ones she enjoyed reading to her daughter. She aims to encourage emotional connection, through meaningful storytelling while building young readers' imaginations.

For more information, free coloring pages, and funny bee riddles, please visit.

https://www.LenaLaRue.com

We hope you enjoyed this book. Please let us and your friends know by leaving a review.

If you liked this book, you might also enjoy PinkyWinky by Lena LaRue and Sammie Clark.

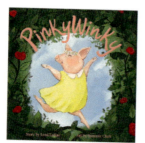

1

Made in the USA
Coppell, TX
25 June 2023